Copyright © MCMLXXXVI by World International Publishing Limited.
All rights reserved.
Published in Great Britain by World International Publishing Limited.
An Egmont Company.
Egmont House, P.O. Box 111, Great Ducie Street, Manchester M60 3BL.
Printed in Belgium. SBN 7235 7159 7.

my first book of animals

words by Brenda Apsley
pictures by David Moss

Some animals live on farms.
How many different animals can you see?

cows

sheep

Farmers keep dairy **cows** for their milk.
Butter and cheese are made from milk.
Cows eat grass.

Baby cows are called calves.

Beef cattle are kept for meat.
Large herds are sometimes rounded up by men on horses.

Goats are kept for their milk.
Goats' milk makes good cheese.
Goats eat grass and vegetables, but they will try to eat almost anything!

Baby goats are called kids.

Sheep live in large groups called flocks.
Sheep are kept for meat and wool.
Sheep have soft woolly coats called fleeces.
In summer the woolly fleeces are cut off.
Sheep graze on grass.

Baby sheep are called lambs.

The **sheep dog** is a working animal, not a pet.
The sheep dog helps the farmer to move the
sheep from one place to another.
The dog obeys the farmer's whistles and shouts.

Dogs sometimes help farmers to move cattle, too.

Some birds are kept on farms. How many different birds can you see?

turkeys

chickens

Turkeys are big birds.

Chickens are kept for eggs.
Chickens live in hen houses.
Chickens eat seeds and grains.

Baby chickens are called chicks.

Ducks are kept for the eggs they lay.
Ducks are good swimmers.
Ducks eat grains and greens.

Baby ducks are called ducklings.

Geese are good swimmers, too.
They lay big eggs.

Baby geese are called goslings.

Dogs come in all shapes and sizes.
Dogs make very good pets.
Dogs are loyal, and love to play.
They wag their tails when they are pleased.
Dogs eat meat and special dog food and biscuits.

Baby dogs are called puppies.
A family of puppies is a litter.

Cats have soft, silky fur, and like to be stroked.
Cats purr when they are happy.
Cats eat meat and fish, and like to drink milk.
Cats are very playful.

Baby cats are called kittens.
Kittens like to chase things.

Ponies are smaller than horses, and are kept for riding.
Ponies need a stable to live in, and a field to run in.
Ponies eat oats and hay, and drink water.
They like carrots, too!

Baby ponies are called foals.
Foals have long, long legs!

Do you know what this pet is?
It's a donkey.

Rabbits have long ears, big feet, and a fluffy white tail.
Pet rabbits live in hutches.
Rabbits eat greens, grains and vegetables.

Baby rabbits are called kits,
though you may call them bunnies!

Some small pets live in cages and tanks.
Do you have a small pet?
Some schools keep small class pets.

hamster

guinea pig

goldfish

mouse

tropical fish

canary

Hamsters are good small pets.
They live in cages with a play area.
They make a bed in soft straw.
Hamsters eat grains, salads and vegetables.
They collect food in their cheek pouches,
and store it to eat later.
Hamsters enjoy using exercise wheels.

Mice like running on exercise wheels, too.
Pet mice are usually white, but there are black and brown ones, too.
Mice eat grains and vegetables.

Guinea pigs live in large cages with soft straw beds.
Guinea pigs eat grains and greens.
They are sometimes called cavies.

Goldfish are very easy pets to keep. They like clean water in their tanks, and eat special fish food.
Tropical fish need more care. They live in special heated tanks.

Small birds are popular pets.
Do you know what this little yellow bird is?
It's a **canary**.
Canaries like to sing.
They eat seeds and greens.

Some animals live in parks and gardens. They are wild animals, but are used to people. How many can you see?

pigeons

squirrel

swans

sparrows

Pigeons are plump, clever birds.
Pigeons eat grains, seeds and scraps.
They can be very tame.

Squirrels live in large gardens and parks.
They are active animals with long, bushy tails.
Squirrels eat insects, seeds and nuts.
Squirrels live in nests.

Sparrows are small brown birds.
They are very common in towns and cities.
Sparrows eat seeds and scraps.

Swans are large water birds.
They have white feathers and long necks.
Baby swans are called cygnets.

**Some animals live in zoos.
These animals and birds spend a lot of their time in water, and are good swimmers.**

penguins

dolphins

Polar bears are big, strong animals — much taller than a man.
Polar bears have very thick, warm fur.
They are good swimmers.
Polar bears hunt seals and fish for food.
In the wild, they live in cold, icy lands.

Baby polar bears are called cubs.

Seals are clumsy on land, but they are very good swimmers.
Seals can stay under water for up to half an hour.
Seals eat fish.

Baby seals are called pups.

Penguins are birds that cannot fly.
They can swim very well, and catch fish to eat.
In the wild, most penguins live in cold, icy lands.
They live in large groups, called colonies or rookeries.

Dolphins are the most intelligent water animals.
They live in large groups called schools.
Dolphins eat fish.
In zoos, dolphins can be taught to do tricks.

Some land animals live in zoos or wildlife parks. Have you seen any of these animals, in a zoo or on television?

Elephants are the largest of all land animals.
Elephants have very long noses called trunks.
Elephants can smell, drink, feed themselves and pick up things with their trunks.
Elephants eat grass, leaves and berries.

Baby elephants are called calves.

Giraffes are the tallest land animals.
They are taller than three men!
Giraffes look clumsy, but they can run very fast.
Giraffes eat twigs and leaves, which they strip
from trees with their long, strong tongues.

A baby giraffe is as tall as a man.

Bears are very big, strong animals.
They move quickly, and are good climbers.
Bears eat fish, small animals and berries.
They also love honey!

Baby bears are called cubs.

Chimpanzees are very clever animals, and love to play.
They are good climbers, and swing from tree to tree.
Chimpanzees eat eggs, fruits, insects and vegetables.
Baby chimpanzees cling to their mothers.

Lions are strong and fierce.
They hunt animals for food.
Lions live in family groups, called a pride.
The male lion has a thick mane of fur around its neck.

Baby lions are called cubs.
A group of cubs is a litter.

Kangaroos have large, strong back legs, small front legs, and long, thick tails.
They move very fast, by hopping and leaping.
Kangaroos eat herbs and grasses.
They live in groups called mobs.

Baby kangaroos are called joeys.
They live in their mother's pouch until they are old enough to look after themselves.